"You're the strongest person you know. All you have to do is be real and honest and people will love you. People admire strength. I used to be as delicate as a flower, but now I'm one of the strongest people I know."

This book is dedicated to everyone who has helped me through my journey, encouraged me, told me they admired me and wanted to hear more from me.

The Beginning

The twelve year old boy was running late to his math class. He had gym class right before math and was now hurrying late to class. He had just changed his shoes at his locker and was heading to his classroom, which was conveniently located near his locker. However, it was January and there was snow on the ground outside which had been tracked inside by the students.

A puddle of melted snow on the floor was all it took for the young-twelve year old boy to lose his footing. As he slipped and fell it was in a quite queer position landing on his left leg. He fell in a position that looked like he was kneeling. He then proceeded to fall completely. He lay on the floor moaning in pain while one of his shoes remained on his foot and the other flew off a few feet away.

Two teachers were in the hallway talking to each other in clear view of the boy who fell. At first, they could not hear the boy's cries of pain. But after a few moments they heard the young boy and rushed over to his side. They came over to the boy and started saying words to him, but the boy could not comprehend their words all the way. His ears were filled with the immense throbbing pain in his leg. All of a sudden the boy's math teacher emerged from a classroom and rushed next to his side. There she met the other two teachers who had already begun comforting the boy. The boy just laid on the floor in excruciating pain as the three teachers crowded around him. One kneeled down and held the boy's hand telling him to squeeze it as hard as he wanted to mask some of the pain the boy was experiencing. In what felt like hours on end, but in reality was only a minute or so, the school nurse arrived with a wheelchair.

The wheelchair was placed beside the boy who laid on the floor and the nurse and teachers proceeded slowly and carefully to lift the boy into the wheelchair. The teachers watched as the nurse took the boy into the elevator and upstairs towards her office. In the nurse's office, the boy's leg was swollen, puffy and grew to about twice its size.

The nurse called the boy's father and in a matter of

minutes his father was there. The nurse told the boy and his father that it was probably a ripped tendon or something less severe than a completely broken leg. The young boy was shocked by this statement. Sure he was only twelve, never had a broken bone before, and the nurse *is* a nurse, licensed and surely qualified, but the boy could not help but believe it was more than that. The boy and his father set out in somewhat of a rush to the emergency room of the old hospital. The entire way the boy's swollen leg kept throbbing with tremendous pain as if someone was hitting it with a hammer repeatedly over and over again.

The Longest Ride

The hospital was only a few minutes away but again to the boy minutes during this event felt like hours. The two of them finally reached the hospital emergency room where the boy waited in the car while his father got a wheelchair from inside. The father carefully transferred the boy out of the car seat and wheeled him into the emergency room. They were greeted by a young lady at the desk who asked the boy and father's information with a rather calm and monotone voice. She asked the boy and his father several question before allowing them inside.

In a couple more long minutes they were let in through the side door of the glass cubicle-like area where the lady sat behind the desk. The nurse started by taking the boy's temperature, blood pressure, and all the basics for any nurse's procedure. Then she asked the boy his pain level. The pain level was based on a one to ten scale. One, being the least amount of pain and ten, the worst. The nurse described it as one was the equivalent of hitting your hand and ten being someone who just got in a major car accident and broke his or her legs. The boy thought about it for a few moments and answered with a pain level or six or seven. He hesitated on both numbers, but ended up choosing and telling the nurse he decided on a six. The nurse wrote down some notes and shortly thereafter the boy and his father were taken to the back of the emergency room where the actual patient rooms were located.

The Most Patient 12 year Old

The boy was in a small room for a short amount of time before he was taken to get x-rays to determine the extent of his leg damage. The x-rays were taken and the boy was sent back to his little room. There he and his father waited for the results to be processed and examined by an ER doctor. The boy thought it was probably an extremely, bad broken leg, but he could not possibly fathom what his father was thinking.

When you are a kid you can not possibly imagine what a parent feels when their son or daughter is hurt. So, the boy sat there quietly waiting for his results. He sat there in a way that was extremely patient and unexpected for a twelve year old. He stared back and forth from the hospital bed, to his leg and to his father. Time was back into it's rightful feeling and the boy felt the fifteen or twenty minutes that went by as real time. Finally a doctor arrived with the boy's x-rays.

The doctor had determined from the x-rays that the boy had a golf ball sized tumor on the boy's upper leg bone. From a simple x-ray they could not tell if the tumor is cancerous or benign (meaning non-cancerous). The boy was only twelve, nowhere close to grown up or able to recognize the seriousness of what the doctor just said. But, the boys father who was fifty years of age and was able to recognize the seriousness of the doctor's diagnosis. The father seemed a little taken back by the information, but overall his face was blank, in reality, the father was always good at masking his emotions.

The Part Left Out

What was failed to be mentioned earlier was that the young boy's left leg had been hurting for the last two weeks prior to the fall. Everyday the boy complained about his leg to his dad, teachers, and other family members. However, his cries of pain where not met with much seriousness. This is not because the boy was being ignored, but it was because his father was unemployed, out of work for a while now and did not have the money to take his son to the doctor.

See, the father, the boy, and the boy's brother had already been living with the boy's grandmother for the last couple of years due to lack of money. The father had been unemployed for a while and was leaning on his mother financially. So, the boy's needs were unmet and the father pushed aside the boy's pain each and everyday saying "I don't have the money to take him to the hospital."

Also, the boy's brother was a terrible child and treated the boy's cries of pain with a form of punishment. The brother was only a year older than the boy and he was in all aspects the definition of a problem child. The brother's punishment of the boy consisted of sever beatings as only a brother so close in age could do. The brother would insist that the boy was "faking it", and accused the boy of making up an excuse for attention. But each and every time the boy protested saying it was true the brother only beat him up and drove him to tears.

Bathroom Troubles

The boy was sent home from the hospital in a splint, a soft-like cast around the boy's leg made out of padding and cloth. The boy was also referred to Rush Hospital in Chicago. There, the doctors would be able to assess the boy's condition and he would receive specialized treatment. The two of them went home that night and a couple of days later they'd be going to the hospital.

It was the day of the trip to the city. That morning, the boy was experiencing problems and told his father that he had to go to the bathroom. The boy could not get on the toilet by himself. So, with extreme effort and hardship the boy and his father made it to the bathroom where the boy sat on the toilet. But now for the oddest-unknown reason the boy could not physically go the bathroom and the father yelled at the boy in frustration.

The boy sat there in shock not understanding how his father could yell at him for not producing a bowel movement. Then, at that moment, the boy was starting to feel the frustration radiating off his father.

Rush University Medical Center

The boy got off the toilet and got ready for the long trip to the hospital. The father loaded his son into the truck. This made the boy feel as if he was a sack of groceries or a box of supplies that needed to be packed into the back of the truck.

Nevertheless, both of them were in the truck and their long journey to the non-conveniently located hospital in the city began. After a long and vicious trip, the boy and his father arrived at their destination. The hospital was located right off of an exit, it was enormous to the twelve year old boy's eyes. To this day, that enormous-red building was forever imprinted into the boy's memory.

The inside of the parking garage of the hospital was equivalent to a giant corn maze. The hospital's garage was filled with numerous levels of parking and the boy and his father seemed to go in a never ending circle of levels. Up and up they went to where they finally found a parking spot. The father parked his truck and then got out and helped the boy out of the car. This time the boy had his own wheelchair because his father had rented one knowing it was going to be used several times in the near future. Now the boy was reduced to being pushed around. It was as if the boy was handicapped or an old person, completely unable or equipped with the skills to take care of himself.

Infected

The proceeding future events would prove to change the boy's life forever. After analysis of the tumor it was clearly evident it was infected with cancer. At the realization of this evidence the boy was assigned a specialist who was a pediatric doctor who specialized in cancer treatment. This doctor went over the results of the biopsy and ruled that the cancer was clearly Osteosarcoma. Osteosarcoma is the most common bone cancer. At this stage of the journey, the boy would have never anticipated the sequence of events and the severity of the upcoming ten months that were about to consumer his life.

Dr. Kent

After meeting the doctor, who's name was by the way Dr. Kent, the boy ultimately thought right away how his name rhymed with the word tent. This caused the smallest of chuckles inside the boy's head.

Dr. Kent was a partially bald man, very tall, and had a corny sense of humor. He had a goofy, big smile that distinguished him more as a person than his height or corny jokes. Large bags were noticeable under his eyes which must have been due to lack of sleep and the work of a doctor.

He informed the boy and his father that the next nine months or so would be long, grueling, hard and extremely difficult. Dr. Kent then continued to show the two of them a somewhat drawn out plan for the next several months. The plan was easily comprehensible but highly intricate at the same time. The boy would begin the rigorous process of chemotherapy. This is where bags of *poison* would be pumped into the boy's body to target the cancer and stop the cancer from possibly spreading.

The plan was easy: give the boy two different types of chemo, alternating the two, each two weeks apart from each other. The boy would be given the poison for a couple of months to weaken the cancerous tumor before it would be removed from his leg.

After the doctor's plan was expressed to the boy and his father, the two were sent to get a *real* cast for the boy, since the previous hospital's idea to put him in just a splint was idiotic and met with harsh laughs from the individuals at the Rush hospital. At Rush they knew what real healthcare was suppose to be.

As the boy waited for his new cast, he was asked what color he would like. The boy responded "blue" with a smile since it was his favorite color. Even in the darkest time the boy found some happiness, something to smile about. That's how you know children are truly pure, when the factors of the outside world do not entirely mask over their inborn carefree attitudes and happiness

Chemotherapy

Soon after the blue cast was applied, the boy experienced his first chemo treatment. A permanent intravenous catheter was put into the boy's chest since it would be used frequently. Regular hand IVs are only temporary, only good roughly for about three to five days.

The boy laid in the hospital bed in his room. There he waited while bags of chemo, or as he and his father referred to them as poison, were slowly pumped into his veins. As he watched the fluid drip, the boy found himself unprepared for the upcoming sickness.

He felt nauseous, weak, sleepy, and other emotions and afflictions that were not able to be expressed. He often puked and needed to have a bowl always handy by his bed for when he had to vomit. This was just one treatment of about twenty the boy would experience in the future. This treatment took about a day and the half. This brand of poison took a little over twenty hours to pump into the boy's body. When his treatment was finished the boy and his father climbed back into the truck. They were both tired and the chemo made the boy extremely sleepy.

The aftermath effects of the chemo seemed even worse then during the actual treatment. The chemo's effects actually lasted days after the pumping of the fluid into the boy's chest. For days and days the boy laid around feeling nauseous, occasionally throwing up and feeling completely engulfed into his disease. He began to feel like he could do nothing but just lie there. During his chemo treatments, his life would consist of sleep and feeling pain then shortly afterwards throwing up.

His chest felt like it was slowly collapsing into his heart. The chemo was pumped straight into his chest through the IV. His chest seemed to be losing strength as it began pushing up against his heart.

Probably one of the worst feelings the boy had experienced was dry heaving. The point where your body wants to throw up, but nothing is present in your stomach to be thrown up. Every time this happened to the boy it felt like a million knives were tearing at his throat and stomach. Again with ignorance the boy didn't know that every time he went through chemo he would feel this way. The boy was in for some of the most severe pain of his life.

Incorrectly Labeled

Chemo. Medicine it is called. But really it should be labeled… "toxin." For all of the numerous ways it sucks life from a person's body. Due to the chemo, the boy's body lost vitamins and minerals the body needs to stay in a state of equilibrium. The boy was now on an everyday regime of numerous pills. Just counting and keeping up with the medicine was exhausting. See the pill regime consisted of thirteen pills a day to be taken at three different meals. The pills consisted of magnesium, potassium and phosphorus. Most days the boy had trouble remembering to take all thirteen pills. Taking them was a chore and was viewed with much distaste.

Round 2

About two weeks later it was time for the boy to go back to the hospital and get his next round of chemo. This time his chemo would be a bag of white almost translucent, liquid. It wouldn't take as much time to pump it into his body like the other chemo but in a way it would take longer. The previous chemo was pumped in and bing, bam, boom, you were done! But this chemo had to be peed out.

Each time the boy had this chemo he had to pee it out. The nurses would test his urine each time to determine the level of this new poison left in his system. The boy was not allowed to leave the hospital until the content of the chemo in his pee was at a certain level. Sometimes this chemo caused the boy to be at the hospital for about three to five days. One time it took six days because the level in his system would not go down to the appropriate level. This new chemo had the benefit of less sickness for the boy than the other chemo, but it kept him at the hospital longer.

Scissors No Longer Cut It

The boy's hair was now falling out at a rapid pace. Each chemo treatment killed more and more of his hair cells leaving less and less hair on his head. Chunks were falling out left and right like he was some dog shedding all the time. He would go to sleep at night with his head resting upon his pillow and when he woke up, his pillow would be covered with hair. Every single inch of his pillow case would be covered with tiny pieces of hair.

The boy's head was starting to have bald spots were clumps of hair once lived. The boy's father said it was time to shave it all off, so it would just be gone and hair wouldn't be all over the place. But the boy said no, because he felt like his own disease would become real the moment all his hair was gone. That's when you know that someone is really sick with a disease. The moment being where all traces of hair is missing from a person's head easily distinguishing them as sick. His face was already warped from the medicine and from being tired and weak all the time, but the hair would be the last piece. The last piece of the wicked disease that was slowly consuming his life.

So one day the boy started to get frustrated. He was tired of all his hair falling out and just started to grab at his head. He sat at the edge of his bed and pulled clump after clump off his head to the point where even more bald spots appeared. The boy's father saw the pile of hair on the floor and knew what the boy had been doing and ordered the boy's brother to vacuum it up. The father called the boy out on it, he knew the boy had been pulling out his hair, but the boy denied it, but knew his father did not believe him.   This is when the boy knew it was time. The father finally shaved the boy's entire head. The reality finally soaked in for the boy. The moment the last clump of hair touched the floor the boy knew, his disease totally consumed him.

Liquid Hardship

There was another side affect to some of the medications and chemotherapy the boy was receiving. He now developed mouth sores. At first, long, white lines showed up on the inside of his cheeks. Then they transformed into little white, circular craters that appeared in random places around his mouth.

When the boy got these sores it was the most uncomfortable feeling imaginable. It was hard for him to eat because the slightest touch caused his mouth to react unbearably. Even when he would accidentally touch his face or lay on it the wrong way it felt like his mouth had swelled up or he was punched full force in the face.

To prevent these sores, the boy had to swish a liquid around in his mouth twice a day after a particular chemo treatment. The liquid was a pink, smooth, yet unpleasant chunky mixture that had to be kept in the fridge to keep cool. This was one of the things the boy dreaded the most. The liquid was the most disgusting substance the boy had ever tasted. The cold, smooth, yet chunky liquid felt like it slowly crawled down his throat. It was so bad the boy would prefer throwing up over swishing.

One day the boy's cheeks, without warning, swelled up. He looked in the mirror and his cheeks were completely swollen. He thought he looked like a hamster storing food in the side of his cheeks. He looked in the mirror closer and turned the inside of his cheek to face the mirror. He saw these long, lined white sores on the inside of each cheek. The boy's father was at work and the boy did not think of it as that important of news to bother his father with. His grandmother unknowingly made chili that day for dinner and he could not physically eat it. The spiciness alone made him realize there would be no way he could even attempt to eat it.

This was the absolute worst pain his mouth ever had experienced. The boy's father was at work, didn't want to bother him, so he just prayed the swelling would go down.

So, he just lazed on the couch till his father got home. His father looked at him for a mere few seconds and said "This is serious you should have called me." Again they went to the hospital where the boy had to swish that god awful medicine again and receive more medication. Eventually the swelling went away and his mouth was sore free. The boy could not avoid trips to the hospital no matter how much he tried: it was always inevitable. It seemed he was at the hospital more for emergencies or unplanned visits more than he was actually their for planned tests or treatment.

Routine

He was now going days without eating and when the boy's body wanted to throw up but there was nothing. He would just hang his head over the bucket and wait for the heaves to stop. He actually wanted to throw up, since the dry heaving seemed endless, and occasionally it would just end. Sometimes he would just upchuck a little water, which really seemed pointless to the boy. It was like the chemo inside his body was messing with him. If the boy refused to eat, the poison would make him throw up anything in his stomach.

After throwing up so much the boy finally found some relief to his nausea and throwing up in a form of another pill. This pill was the boy's life saver. It stopped the boy's nausea most of the time and even kept him from throwing up sometimes. When the boy felt a little nauseous he would pop one of those pills and in a few minutes, most of the time, he felt better. However, sometimes he'd take the pill and throw up soon afterwards and it really was a waste of a pill.

Merging Tears

    Nausea, puking, heaving and not eating became weekly routines for the boy, sometimes even daily. Therefore, the boy had to find a fix for all his nausea, something to stop himself from throwing up so much. The doctors told him that throwing up brings up this stomach acid with partially digested food. Therefore, stomach acid will slowly destroy the layers in a throat. The dry heaving seemed to be especially worse than actually throwing up. His head felt like it was racing, he was dizzy from just sitting down. He had this yellow, throw-up bucket next to him and with great swiftness the boy purged all into the bowl and still felt like he was going to throw up again.

    Still feeling nauseous he called for his brother to bring him his nausea pill. The brother brought him his pill and left. He opened the pill, held it in his hand, and accidentally dropped it in the bucket of fresh puke. The stench of the puke was one of the worst smells the boy had ever experienced. The boy looked at the puke for several seconds trying to catch a glimpse of the pill. He could not find it and sat there crying, while trying to form the words to tell his brother that he needed another pill. The boy's speech was so interrupted by the sobs and tears that it took him several tries before the boy's brother understood his words and brought him a fresh pill. He took the new pill and swallowed it and soon felt relief from the nausea. Then his grandma came and disposed of the bucket's contents.

The boy couldn't get the image of sitting there, crying over the bucket out of his mind. Leaning his head over the bucket, crying into it to the point where his exceptionally watery tears submerged into the bucket full of puke.

Never Forget

He was now in the hospital days and days at a time. He sat around passing out constantly from the amount of pain and medication. He was on so much medication that it not only helped him but hurt him at the same time. The medication had made it so the boy was unable to go to the bathroom and caused massive hemorrhoids to swell up inside of his body. Each time the boy attempted to go to the bathroom it was met with more pain and failure. It got so bad to the point where the boy did not physically pooh for four days. This caused multiple hemorrhoids to erupt and the boy's mother and father watched as he struggled and begged for relief. The boy's mother yelled and protested for the father to bring in the doctor again to see if there was anything they could do for him. But the boy's father was a logical man and realized that they could do nothing at this point and eventually the boy would be able to go to the bathroom.

The boy struggled time and time again and twisted around in agony waiting for a sign of relief. But what he got wasn't exactly what he'd hope for. See, the boy finally was able to use the bathroom, but at a terrible cost. When he finally used the bathroom, he was reminded of the massive-pulsating hemorrhoids inside of him. His stool was bloody and going to the bathroom left him in so much pain that he screamed in agony. The pain was so intense the boy wanted to pass out. The screaming was so loud people outside of his room could hear him.

    The boy pressed the button to call for the nurse because it was some of the most excruciating pain the boy had ever felt. The nurse quickly injected the boy with a dose of Morphine. It only took the Morphine about fifteen seconds to work and that's when the boy leaned back on the seat. He sat there for a moment and really took a hard look at his situation. His life felt reduced to pain and medication. It was one thing after another, each one getting worse and each time he felt the pain was more severe than the last time. The boy was mostly calm until this point, but it crossed a whole new level. This was a time the boy would never forget.

Wanting A Normal Life

People have the misconception that cancer only does a few things such as make a person's hair fall out, make a person nauseous, weak, etc. But what they don't know is that it does so much more. Cancer treatment attacks all aspects of the body.

The boy had received numerous cancer treatments at this time. Every time he got this one brew of chemo he had to get a shot. The shot was a white blood cell booster called Neulasta. This shot is specially made to supply more white blood cells to an individual undergoing treatment. However, it is not always effective. The boy's white blood cell count was dangerously low after each one of those cancer treatments. When his white blood cell count dropped, a simple cold or germ could give the boy a serious infection. Almost every time the boy had that chemo, he would get that shot, but it hardly ever worked. He usually ended up getting sick and running a high fever. When this happened, the boy had to run to the hospital with his father and get a round of antibiotics. The boy felt that this routine was even more of an inconvenience on his life and overall childhood.

One night the boy was feeling rather hot and was starting to run a high fever. His grandmother knew he had to go to the hospital but his dad was not home from work yet. The boy sat there protesting to his grandma saying he was alright and went back to playing Halo (a video game) with his older brother. Later that night, the boy's father came home from work. The grandma obviously told his father about the fever out of worry for him. So, the father walked into the boy's room where he saw his two sons playing video games. The father told the boy if his fever did not go down soon they would be going to the hospital. The boy agreed since now he was used to unexpected hospital visits. He sat there and continuously sipped cold water, believing in some way it would help the fever go down.

After a while the boy's fever did not go down and his father came in to check on him. He knew he'd be spending another night at the hospital and die a little more to his disease. The boy put down the controller, said goodbye to his brother and sadly went to the hospital. The boy wished for just one night that he could be normal and actually sit down and enjoy playing a video game with his brother. He felt as if a big part of his childhood was being ripped away from him. It seemed to be by the hands of Death himself. A great deal of the time, the boy felt that death itself was near. It was no longer just a wondering thought or way out of everything, but here right now, a real conclusion that was approaching.

Big White Room

The boy felt so secluded and alone. When people finally did come around he usually didn't speak much and distanced himself that much further. At the end of the hall, in the children's wing of the hospital, is a play room open to all young patients who wish to play a board game, a video game, or read a magazine. The play room was run by a group of people who worked at the hospital along with some volunteers. The boy usually avoided the playroom and denied requests from the volunteers and group leaders to come and play. However, one time the boy obliged and went to the room to go and hang out with a young male volunteer.

The boy had been inside the play room before. Not with the volunteers or the group leaders but with his father and brother. He would sit in the play room and use the Xbox and play Halo with his brother as their father watched. The room seemed dull, ordinary and rather odd during the time he was in there with his father and brother. But now there were other young children's voices echoing in the background along with the young male volunteer. The playroom seemed blindingly white and abnormally clean, as if it was a white tunnel going to some location that when reached, the end was total salvation. It was quite odd. The boy usually felt distanced from himself and others and not fully together but now he felt like he was even more alone. It was like some barely remembered hazy dream.

In a daze, the boy played a few games with the young male volunteer and actually started to enjoy himself a little. And as soon as he started enjoying himself even more the young male volunteer had to go and attend to other children and the boy felt an overwhelming sense of being crushed, stomped on repeatedly. This is why the boy never reached out to anyone. Lately when he tried to gain any sense of happiness he always got a quick taste of it and it was slowly torn away from him. This is why being numb was easier. When the boy was numb nothing was crushing or had too much impact or was too much to handle. Everything floated by and seemed to blend together.

Laughter At Laughter

The boy's cast had to be on for months until he got his knee replacement surgery. Therefore, a single cast could not be on for the whole period of time. He had to get it changed a couple times until his surgery. The boy went in one morning to the hospital and got changed into the usual hospital gowns. His orthopedic surgeon would be changing his cast and observing his leg to see if it had changed at all and if a cast would suffice for preservation.

The boy laid in the hospital bed and waited to be taken in for his cast change. They then moved him into a cold corridor filled with many rooms and people, many of whom were circling around his moving bed. The corridor was beyond cold and he felt like a penguin in the arctic. He finally got to a room on the right side of the corridor where several people were in the room waiting for the boy to arrive. The boy was given a medication aimed to knock the boy out but instead it didn't knock the boy out and caused a rather odd event. The boy did not fall asleep like they planned but instead he laughed uncontrollably and he could not stop. The nurses and the doctor stood there laughing at him because the boy could not stop laughing. He chuckled on and on about nothing. The boy was awake the whole time they removed his cast.

They started off by using a small, electric saw to slice off his old cast. After the doctor removed the cast he then examined the boy's leg thrashing it up and down, twisting and turning it in every direction. His orthopedic doctor was very hands on and rough with his patients and he twisted and turned the boy's leg . The boy said "Ow" and the doctor said, "I guess that's not as well off as I thought." The doctor was also supposed to clean the boy's leg off while he was in there. Since the cast had been on for weeks and weeks now the boy's leg was yellow and quite smelly from the cast. The boy was so angry when the doctor did not clean off his leg, but at least he had a new cast which made his leg somewhat cleaner.

"I'm Fine"

The boy reached another difficult situation as if, he didn't have enough already. Now he wasn't able to shower properly. This was because he had his enormous cast on his leg and tubes in his chest. Neither of these two items where allowed to get wet. His cast would get ruined if he got water inside of it. The hole in his chest where the tubes entered had a cover on it, if any water got into the hole, it could cause an infection that would be bad news for the boy.

The boy usually went days without a shower and it was quite grotesque. Even with all the obstacles in his way the boy's clever father did come up with a simple, but mildly painful solution. To protect the boy's tubes from getting wet his father wrapped them up in a zip loc bag, zipped it up, then taped the edges over so it could not get wet. Then his father would take his leg wrap it up in a full-sized thirty gallon garbage bag and tape it up around his leg.

This process was a struggle for the boy and his father,

sounded simple, but it was rather difficult. Finally, the father was done tapping and wrapping the boy like he was a present. It was rather odd for the boy in the shower. He couldn't stand up so he had to use the walk-in shower that was located in his room. See, the boy's handicapped uncle used to live in his room. So, he was lucky to have an installed walk in shower. The boy jumped his way into the shower by hopping on one foot and sat down on the shower chair located in the shower.

The shower was a big open area with a hose for a shower head and a single big drain located off center. It was freezing for the boy inside of the shower, since it was wide and open to the medium-sized bedroom. The boy froze each and every time he used that shower. It was extremely difficult for him to wash up in the shower he could hardly move and shivered the whole time he was in there.

When the boy would get out of the shower he had to unravel the zip loc bag from the tubes on his chest and remove the tape which seemed to almost rip off part of his skin. It made his chest incredibly red and sore for a while. Then he had to pull the tape off his leg which felt like he was ripping a thousand band aids off at once. The boy showered once or twice per week because the long process to get ready for a shower was so much work for the boy and his father. It also didn't hurt that they couldn't afford to waste too many zip loc bags or garbage bags.

At least in some of the awful situations of his life he could drum up some humor. In other times, he, through a fake smile, would repeat the biggest lie in the world…"I'm fine."

Escape Reality

During his stays at the hospital for his chemo treatments the boy would sit around for hours in his room. The hospital television in his room only had a few channels and most of the time nothing good was on. Television wasn't always enough to amuse the boy. Eventually a person needs human interaction and needs to turn the television off. The boy, with enormous effort, would crawl out of his hospital bed and put on a set of real clothes from the drawer in his room. After he dressed, the boy would drag the heavy stand with his bag of medications along side of him and walked out of his room. His room seemed a little stuffy after a while and the clear air from the hallway embraced his lungs.

He walked down to the end of the hallway where the nurses' station was located. It was an open area with a few desks and many chairs where the nurses would eat and take down their notes in their binders. Also enclosed at the nurse's station was a big board with every patients name, what room number their in, gender, age, and the name of the nurse assigned to that patient.

The boy would sit down at the nurse's station and try to have some interaction with his nurse and the other nurses.

The nurses at Rush were some of the nicest people ever, but the boy knew they were quite busy and could only amuse him for a while, because really he wasn't supposed to be in there. The boy just craved for some attention. He would sit in his room alone for days in the dark with little interaction with anyone. The only interaction he had was when his nurse would come in from time to time to give him medication or take blood for testing. Knowing that the nurses were busy and had no extra time for him, knowing he wasn't supposed to be there at the nurse's station, the boy slowly hunched over and walked back to his room.

He walked back so slowly that the hallway seemed endless and now that he thought of it, the hallway was really white and the lights were rather bright, like he was walking down the long white tunnel to salvation. The boy finally reached his room dragging his heavy medicine stand behind him and slowly crawled back into bed and threw the covers over himself. He was back by himself again. Alone again in his dark, empty room. He went back to the realization of loneliness and tried to fall asleep to escape his depression and more important, escape reality.

Mrs. Byrne

The boy would be in and out of the hospital for the next several months so school wasn't an option for him. He had to drop out of school and get a private tutor. The first lady they sent over was a teacher from his school. She was old with a bitter personality. She appeared rather odd looking and wore outdated clothes coupled with her flat, dry looking hair. Her warped face made her an unattractive person. She came in basically insulting the boy's family, saying his father and grandmother smoked too much and she wanted to take the boy out to a different location to do the tutoring. His dad went and complained to the school shortly afterwards and the boy received a new tutor.

His new tutor ended up being his science teacher Mrs. Byrne. A middle aged woman, with a shade of blonde hair never before seen by the boy. The boy was ecstatic with the replacement, since Mrs. Bryne was one of his favorite teachers. She was cool, easy going, and fun to be around. She'd come to the boy's house for tutoring two to three times a week. She still had to teach her science class at the middle school, but was making a little extra money tutoring the boy.

The two to three days a week was proving to not be enough tutoring, because a great deal of the boy's work was going undone and the boy's grades dropped. The boy had always been an A and B student, but due to missing school and not having enough tutoring the boys grades dropped to B's and C's. This wouldn't seem too bad for most kids, especially doing school work while battling a disease, but the boy had always prided himself on his achievements in school. So, when the boy saw his grades he was extremely upset and actually blamed Mrs. Bryne for not being able to come to his house enough for tutoring.

The boy also grew more and more suspicious of Mrs. Bryne the more time they spent together. Occasionally, the boy and the teacher would go out and see a movie with the boy or do some shopping. Every once in a while it was good for the boy to just get out of the house and feel somewhat normal. The inside of his room and lonely hospital stays had became too reoccurring for the boy to handle. He needed fresh air, car rides and to see new places. However, the boy began to realize, with some of his dad's help, and because he wasn't as naïve as some people, that part of Mrs. Byrne's new job description was to keep the boy and his family happy. Happy because the school could be sued for liability. The school and the school district were probably too afraid of the possibility that the boy and his family would sue the school.

So, in his mind, the boy questioned whether his teacher had really befriended him or was she simply trying to avoid a lawsuit against the school. The thoughts became a different image of what the boy previously believed. This scared him and frustrated him. Was she really that conniving? It also upset the boy because he finally felt the presence of a friend. A friend he had been excited to see. But now he suspected she was a fake. A fake stage doll created by the school to ensure that the boy and his family remain "happy."

White Castle Mom

Growing up the boy never had a good relationship with his mother. He never saw much of her over the years and was mildly surprised when she came to visit him at the hospital. When she would come she would spend the night because the boy's mother lived a couple hours away from the hospital.

One time the mother came to visit the boy and asked him if he wanted White Castle. The boy said yes to White Castle because he could not eat the hospital food. The chemotherapy already made the boy nauseous and the smell of the hospital food made the boy even more nauseous. At one point, it got so bad that the nurse had to post a sign on the boy's hospital room door that said "no food tray."

When the boy was at the hospital to get his new poison, he could only eat outside fast food or food from the hospital restaurant. The boy's mom went to get White Castle and returned not long afterwards. The boy began to eat the White Castle burgers and got weird feelings in his stomach and throat. He couldn't believe it. He couldn't even eat any kind of food anymore. At this point the boy already looked as if he was loosing weight and color was draining from his face. He illuminated a strong white, pale complexion that made him resemble an albino.

His mother asked him why he wasn't eating more of his food and the boy responded by saying he wasn't feeling that well and couldn't stomach eating anymore. The boy sat there wanting to eat the few White Castle burgers sitting in front of him, but could not get himself to eat them.

That night the mother fell asleep next to the boy's bed in a giant, green and cushy chair that reclined. The boy's mother was small and she could of easily fit three times her body size into that chair. She laid stretched out on the recline couch, her small and tired body compressing against the chair. The boy fell asleep that night not completely alone since his mother was there right next to him. He couldn't stop recalling one night from a month before. The boy had troubles going to the bathroom. He was on his fourth day of not going to the bathroom. He remembered being so stuffed up from all the medicine he was on and he could not go to the bathroom. Over and over again he remembered how his mother cried and screamed for the boy's father to go call a doctor in to see about his troubles going to the bathroom. He'll never forget that moment.

Mrs. Holloway and the Video

One day, Mrs. Holloway came in to see the boy at his house. She had been his language arts teacher at the school before he broke his leg. The point of her visit was to shoot a video for Meadowdale Elementary School. There was a charity event for the boy and Mrs. Holloway simply wanted a personal thank you, from the boy. It was March 2005. This was only two months after the boy was diagnosed with cancer,

The boy had gotten home from the hospital the day before she arrived and he wasn't feeling very well. He really didn't want to do the video. It's not that he was ungrateful in any way, he was awfully tired and felt the utmost sickness stirring inside him. It was obvious how sick the boy appeared. He was now completely bald. He had no hair at all, not even eyebrows or eyelashes. The chemo treatment had been effecting his skin. The boy had dark spots on his head, where his skin was dried out and where he had been scratching and he still looked like an albino. If that wasn't enough, the boy faced the problem of ordinary pubescent effects.

The one ordinary thing the boy could experience as a child and it was acne.

The video ended up being multiple questions from Mrs. Holloway, such as "What's up with your leg", "Do all the kids on that hospital floor have cancer", "Miss school?" The boy answered all these questions as he looked at the ground. He looked straight at Mrs. Holloway and the video camera only a couple times and when he did, it was for only a quick second. He felt so sick and didn't want to be there. Mrs. Holloway, even though across the living room, pointed the camera at his face. It was like she was documenting every moment of the boy's life. But what really was the boy's life? It was an encumbrance of sorrow, pity, loathing, hate, tears, pain, torture. Why did it seem to be so glorifying? Why did she stick a camera in front of the boy's and document his life?

After two months it was already too much for the boy too handle. It was an overly excessive amount of crap on the boy's frail shoulders. How is a twelve year old boy supposed to understand and cope with everything that is happening and unraveling in front of his eyes.

Easter Will Never Be the Same

Easter was around the corner and the boy had entered the hospital again. The boy knew whenever he went into the hospital he'd be there for days and he would miss Easter this year. He thought about all the great food he would be missing since his grandmother made a delicious-moist ham every year accompanied with savory potato salad and other treats. The boy sat around Easter day rather bummed, a little depressed, and missing the food and more important the presence of his father. He was yet again alone, but even more depressing, alone on a holiday.

However, the next day the father had a little surprise for him. The father brought containers of all the left overs from Easter dinner. The boy rustled around back and forth in his bed and gave his father a massive hug, which was quite odd seeing how the boy had little strength to draw that energy forward after not eating for days and only having a little water. The boy sat there happily eating his food and sitting down talking to his father. It was like they were having there own little Easter party which actually felt better to the boy, since his grandmother is a rather grouchy person and yells often.

Everything was just dandy until about fifteen minutes after the boy was done eating. He all of a sudden felt sick and knew what was going to happen. He quickly stretched out his arm and grabbed the bucket next to his bed. He then spewed vomit everywhere as his father watched. The boy thought, 'Hey I got to eat it and take on none of the weight, what a win-win." But really the boy was tired of vomiting all the time. It may not sound that bad, but to him there is nothing worse.

The father seemed taken aback more by this, then the boy and called a doctor in and told him what had just happened. All the doctor could say was to recommend more pills to try and prevent nausea and vomiting. Sometimes after the boy vomited he would just sit there, no expression on his face what so ever, and just gaze at his trusty bucket. Most people would be grossed out and quickly try to dispose of it, but not the boy. He felt intense misery after throwing up, like it was the central axis of everything. Sometimes it felt like he stared at the vomit in the bucket for minutes. His face never changing, his body still, then he would finally come back to reality and have someone toss it away. Every time they did, it was like the boy lost a part of himself, in some sick and disgusted way that puke was him slowing fading away.

One Hell Of A Drug

Not everything is so clear to the boy all the time. He felt so disorientated from the medicine. At times, it didn't seem like he was inside his body but floating above himself looking down at his unmoving body. One time, the boy was allowed a morphine machine to counterattack his mild to moderate pain. He received an advance dose of morphine and was allowed to push a button to release more morphine every eight minutes. The boy was now somewhat addicted to morphine and used it to escape the pain of his current situation and overall reality.

Morphine is one HELL of a drug and was the boy's equivalent for heroin. The boy hit that eight button like clockwork staring at the clock counting every eight minute interval. Not only did the boy hit the button every eight minutes but then proceeded to ask the doctor for an extra dose and the doctor easily obliged. He ended up having so much morphine pumped through is veins he blacked out.

He awoke several hours later disorientated, unaware of

what had happened and even where he was. In reality he was only asleep for a couple of hours but it felt like a week to the boy. On top of everything he had something new to worry about: his overall dependency on morphine to escape his life. It became easier to drop below his conscious level, feeling nothing and just lay there and be numb. Being numb was easier.

Wasting Away Time

February, March, and April went by at a glacial pace. Each day seemed to be dragging on. The boy was exhausted and tired all the time. All the back and forth trips to the hospital were exhausting. An hour to the hospital, then off to admitting to get a wristband and a hospital room on the fifth floor. Next, up to the fifth floor where he would tell the nurses at the nursing station that they arrived, followed by one of the nurses escorting him to his room. Meeting his nurse for the night and soon enough starting his chemo treatment. The boy would be there anywhere from two days to about a week, depending on the chemo treatment he was receiving.

    The boy spent most of his time pinned to his bed, wasting away. After numerous doses of chemo, unwanted infections due to his limited number of white blood cells, uncountable upchucks of vomit and so much more, it was finally time for the boy to get the surgery that would change his life forever.

The Day That Changed Everything

It was just a regular day in May. The sun was up like any other day and a surgery would make any normal person afraid, worried, and such, but not the boy, he was rather happy that the day was finally here. The surgery was very early in the morning and the boy had to wake up quite early since the hospital was an hour away.

When they arrived at the hospital he registered for his surgery with his dad and they sat down. After a while they called his name and the boy was prepped for surgery. He changed into a gown and was taken on a rolling bed down the elevator to the operating floor.

After sitting in the cold room in his hospital gown under mountains of covers waiting and waiting, they finally came for him. He was taken to the operating room by several people each grabbing the bars around the bed. They then drugged the boy and he fell into a great sleep.

While asleep he knew what they were going to do. A

month or so before the surgery the boy and his father met with the boy's orthopedic surgeon (the bone doctor). He was an older looking, balding and gray man. He was blunt and he didn't tip toe around things. He demonstrated to the boy and his dad what he'd be doing during the surgery. The femur bone that the tumor had been in was no longer good and had to be partially removed from the boy's body. As he explained, when a normal bone breaks most of the time you can set it back in place and it will heal in a few weeks. When the boy's bone broke it was infected with cancer and it weakened the bone which had to be replaced with a whole new bone and knee. The replacement would be a long metal rod that had the same appearance and quality of a knee and upper leg bone.

    During the surgery, the bone doctor and the other nurses and surgeons cut a slit on the boy's left leg over a foot long so they could remove the infected bone and replace it with the metal knee replacement. One and a half muscles had to be removed from the boy's knee to be able to fit the knee replacement in. This left the boy's knee disfigured and hideous. The surgery took over seven hours. The boy woke up in the recovery room with his father looking down upon him. His father wasn't the most emotional person and wasn't very expressive, but his love was evident and clear. His father never left his side and was there with the boy through everything.

Helplessness

For the next week or two the boy could hardly move. He spent most of his time in the hospital somewhat pampered by the nurses. The boy couldn't get up to go to the bathroom, so he had a catheter placed in his penis that emptied into a bag. He also had to have a nurse place a bed pan under him whenever he had to pooh. The boy called his nurse the first few times he had to pooh, but it made him feel helpless, like he couldn't do anything himself. The next time he had to go pooh he tried to lift himself up and put the pan under himself and pooh. But the boy ending up not putting it under himself quite right and ended up poohing all over himself and his bed. He ended up having to call the nurse. The young boy was so embarrassed and upset. The nurse had to help the boy out of the bed and change the sheets. The nurse was angry with the boy because he did not call her when he should have and she now had extra work to do. Her speech to him was angry and was received as bitter by the boy

But all the boy wanted was to finally do something by

himself. To stop depending on people to service him was one thing he wanted the most. He was tired of crapping in a bed pan, peeing in jars and puking in buckets. He just wanted it all to end. Going to the bathroom like a normal person was one thing he wished for the most. But one of his biggest wishes was to stop puking. Every time the boy puked it felt like he was losing a piece of himself. Every time he puked, a piece of himself died in the bucket along with the vomit.

Unwanted Service

The boy lied there in waiting. Bored, out of his mind, nothing to do. Just empty time to sit around watching the IV slowly pump *medicine* into his sunken chest. One might think being waited on by people is the greatest thing in the world, however the boy would give anything just to be able to do things himself. Again, after his surgery, he could no longer go to the bathroom by himself, reach certain things or go long distances without a wheelchair. He felt imprisoned. Chained and bound to a rough, slightly stiff hospital bed, at the mercy of others. Being sick and secluded wasn't enough, now his independence was mostly gone.

A New Challenge

The boy had weeks of physical therapy to do. He had to meet with the hospital physical therapist twice a day and each time he met with her he hated it. It was tortuous to the boy. It was like he had to learn to walk all over again. He felt like an injured sick puppy that needed assistance with everything. The boy had to stand up and walk along these parallel bars to teach himself how to walk again. The pain seared up and down the boy's legs with each and every step he took. If the chemotherapy wasn't enough now the boy had to deal with the constant leg pain.

One time the boy went down to the physical therapy room of the hospital and was extremely embarrassed. He sat on one of the beds in his hospital gown and when he stood up there was pooh stains all over the bed sheet. The boy was utterly embarrassed when he got up to begin his leg training. One of the physical therapist clearly saw the stain, cleaned up the sheets and put new fresh ones onto the bed. The boy was paralyzed with embarrassment. He wished at that moment he could run out of the room and avoid everyone who had just seen what he had done. But there was no possible way that he could run, he could barely walk. He was trapped in that room for the next half hour, and it reminded him of every minute of what just happened to him.

Now that the boy's surgery was done and physical therapy was started he was able to go home and recover more. While at home, they arranged for a physical therapist to go to the boy's house once or twice a week to assist in the boy's recovery. Along with the physical therapist a machine was sent to the boy's house. The machine was designed to stretch and advance the flexibility of the boy's leg. The machine was set to a range of flexibility and each day the range was set to the next level. The end point was when the leg finally flexed all the way like the other leg. The boy's left leg was basically new after the surgery but he could hardly bend it at all. Over a period of two weeks, the combined effort of the machine and the physical therapist stretched the boy's leg to it's maximum flexibility. Now that was one less thing for the boy to worry about but his dad had a new problem.

The insurance company was refusing to pay for the machine's use for the last two weeks. The bill ended up being two thousand dollars and after all the medical bills the boy and his father had already they could not possibly afford that kind of money. Eventually after months of arguing the boy's father got the bill all settled and the insurance company paid for every cent of the bill.

Butterfly Band-Aids

Two weeks after the surgery the boy had to go back to the hospital and have his staples removed. Most people generally get stitches after surgery or an accident, but the boy had to get staples on his leg. These were not ordinary staples. These staples were as thick as if you put four staples together. Over the staples were white, thin, long strips of band aids that were called butterfly band aids.

The boy had forty of these staples lined up his leg. His orthopedic doctor told the boy he could take out some of his own staples if he wanted to. To take out the staple he was given a giant version of a staple remover. The boy sat there and took out some of his staples one by one. Each time he removed a staple it felt as if someone had pinched him the hardest they could. After doing a few staples the boy could no longer do anymore and asked the doctor to finish the rest. So the doctor sat there for another few minutes plucking the boy's staples out of his leg one at a time as if he was plucking someone's eyebrows. When the doctor was finally done removing the staples you could see tiny bumps all over the boy's leg. The boy felt relieved when the doctor was finally done removing the staples. It slowly felt better but the huge and ugly scar left behind measured out to be a little bit bigger than a foot.

Scar

Every night the boy would lie up at late hours of the night and stare at his scar. He stared at the huge and ugly line that covered a good portion of his leg. Every night he would think of how could this of happened to him, of how he was left with such an ugly, disfiguring scar. He knew now that every time someone would see his scar they would be revolted and ask what happened. He did not want to be faced with this for the rest of his life. His doctor assured the boy that in time the scar would heal and become less and less noticeable, just like normal scars. It didn't matter how many times the boy heard this or who he heard it from, he could not get over the ugly site.

Many nights when the boy would lie up at night and stare at his scar he would also cry. He would sit up, bend his knees as if trying to curl up in a ball and cry. Tears dripped down his face in the size of bullets and fell upon his body. Why did this happen to me? The boy would say over and over again while crying. Who is going to love me when I look like this?

Most nights the boy sat up and said these things aloud to himself. It didn't matter if he was home in his bed or in a hospital room receiving another round of chemo: the boy would stare at his scar for at times longer than an hour and just think about what the rest of his life was about to look like. He imagined himself alone, crying, with no one able to love him because they could never get over his ugly, disfigured leg.

What Is Fair

Now that the boy was in and out of the hospital and sick most of the time, his brother had to pick up all the chores the boy used to do. The boy's brother complained and acted rather selfish. Would you rather be sick almost all the time, in and out of hospitals or do some extra chores for a few months? This is exactly what the boy thought. The boy's brother complained so much that the boy's father began to agree with him. The father now made the boy get up and wash dishes. Stand there, with terrible balance, and wash the dishes to satisfy the brother. The boy however realized it was fair and he stood there and washed the dishes and laughed at how he could barely stand up.

The Heat On the Day of the Baseball Game

As the months of May and June went on the boy had to face a new obstacle. That obstacle was the heat of summer. One day Meadowdale Elementary School was having a benefit for him. The benefit was a local elementary school baseball game where half of the proceeds would go to the boy's family. The boy arrived that day with his father and the rest of his extended family.

Where they had to park was far away to where the seats were and the boy just finished a round of chemo two hours before the game. The temperature was about ninety degrees that day and the boy had been feeling nauseous and seemed to be gasping for air all the way from the hospital to the baseball field. As his father was helping the boy out of the car the boy was almost wheezing and almost on the verge of tears. The father rather quickly yelled at the boy saying he was whining too much and stop all the noise.

The boy was rather taken aback by this. He just received a round of chemo, and the heat was making him feel even more sick, a sick twelve year old, and his father was yelling at him. The boy whined back in distress telling himself what was he supposed to do. He couldn't control what his body was currently doing.

Both of them, casting it aside, walked down to the field and tried to enjoy the baseball game. The boy put on a fake smile to greet his fellow citizens and donators. Half the money raised was donated to the boy and his family, but as it was a fifty-fifty raffle, the guy who won the other half ended up donating his winnings to the family

The baseball game was overall a success. The boy spent most of the time sitting on the bleachers eating popsicles. However, the boy was starting to feel his dad's misplaced anger and frustration.

Other Benefits

In addition to the baseball benefit game there was a couple other benefits for the boy and his family. There was a charity run for the boy where the students of Lakewood ran around the school like it was a track.

Half of the money raised went to the boy and his family and the other half went towards the school. Another fundraiser that took place was a spaghetti dinner at the school. People would come to the school, pay five dollars for a spaghetti dinner and the money, again like before, would be donated to the boy and his family. The last fundraiser that was conducted for the boy was a pizza dinner. It was virtually the same concept as the spaghetti dinner, instead it was pizza.

The boy really wanted to attend the pizza dinner. He was looking forward to the dinner. However, like all the other times in his life, something unexpected happened. The boy got sick as a result of his treatments and spent the day in the hospital, unable to attend the dinner. Another instance where the boy finally got mildly excited about something and it ended with him alone, in a hospital bed, staring at a black television screen while medicine pumped into his sunken chest.

Reintroduction to School

The rather hot summer that year passed and the boy was finally ready to start school again the following fall for seventh grade. It was the boy's first day at a school in months. He was now at a new middle school, so everything in the school was new to him. However, in some ways it didn't matter that it was a new school. Most of the same people he knew before were now going to the middle school. His story was a local, tragic story, so many of the teachers and students he didn't even know knew him. It's actually kind of odd when so many people know you and know things about your life, but you have absolutely no idea who these people are or anything about them. The boy had forgotten what it was like at school.

The boy struggled from the very beginning. He had trouble walking up the stairs. It took him a long few minutes and several people passed him on his way up. He had to go up a few stairs stop to rest, do a few more, stop, and continue till he got to the top.

Everyone who knew the boy in seventh grade looked and starred at the boy. The chemo treatments had left the boy bald, without hair anywhere on his body. Everyone knew him as the kid with cancer and his bald head made it worse. He felt that he only had friends because they felt bad for him because "you have to be nice to the kid with cancer." That day he went home and told his grandma and dad how hard it was to make it through the day. Walking home from the bus stop to the house was exhausting. It was only a short walk, but to the boy it felt like miles. Even when not in the hospital the boy was limited. His new artificial leg had rendered him slow and weak. But after a week, the young boy got used to it and was happy to be back in school. Being back at school meant that the boy was somewhat normal again. He was excited by the little extra thrill in his life.

The "Sick Kid"

Now being back to school for seventh grade the boy felt odd. He saw all of his old friends but it was not the same. They were his friends but really weren't his friends at the same time. The boy had really missed about six months of school but when he returned for seventh grade everything was different. He thought he was his normal self, a little cheery, a little happy, a mildly okay kid. But his self image was now twisted by his cancer. It seemed like everyone was whispering behind his back "There goes the cancer kid" or "Oh that's why he's bald."

Although no one actually said those words, he knew deep down that maybe, but not forever, at this current point in his life, he would be portrayed as the "sick kid" and "cancer kid." He never wanted to be seen this way, because it wasn't something horrible or distinguishing but a mark imprinted on his forehead that said "broken."

Broken

People stared and looked at the boy perplexed when he would walk by with his limp due to his artificial knee. His slowness almost seemed to be like he was gliding across the hallways and his absence of hair was the most attributing factor to his broken status. He felt utterly alone, secluded and absent from the world. He met their glares and odd looks with ignorance as if he didn't know what they were looking at, but really it was if he could read their minds....*broken*.

The Last One

For the next three months the boy missed school frequently and was still making his trips to the hospital and receiving his treatment. However, in November he finally received his last chemo treatment. He went home that day feeling sick and gross as usual, but felt great at the same time, because he was finally done with chemo. After the next week or so there would be no excessive amount of vomiting, no feeling weak and tired all the time. His hair would eventually grow back and as time would go on he would look less and less broken. Still he was not done with the hospital. He had to go back every couple months to get tests done to make sure no other problems occurred or his cancer did not come back.

Check-ups

Now the boy was done with chemo. His next step was to continue to get check-ups every couple of months. At his check-ups he would undergo x-rays and scans to make sure his cancer did not return. His remission was scheduled for five years beginning after his last chemo treatment which was in Nov of 2005. In those five years he would continue to do have routine hospital visits.

Off the Even Path

New problems continued to pop up for the boy. His legs were uneven. His left leg seemed to be over an inch short and the boy had trouble walking. The boy had grown too much and his left leg didn't have the capacity to grow as much as his right leg after the surgery, which left the boy with a height discrepancy. The boy had to get a shoe made with a lift in it to accommodate for his height difference. People starred at the boy and always asked him what was up with his shoes. The boy eventually became frustrated and so depressed about the shoes that he tricked everyone into believing that he no longer needed the lift. The boy ditched the lift but the stress of one bad thing after another seemed never ending.

8th Grade

The boy had finished seventh grade with many difficulties: treatments, hospital visits, missing school and more. He continued to long for a normal life.

The boy avoided any sort of extra activities in seventh grade. How could he handle all those activities when he had difficulties managing the regular school stuff like homework, projects and tests? This year, he was determined to actually get involved and participate in at least one activity. Now that he was done with the chemotherapy treatments he now had the opportunity to do more at school. He still had check-ups and leg problems, but at least there wasn't any poison invading his body.

At the beginning of the year there were announcements for anyone who wanted to join choir to meet in the choir room during their lunch. So the boy went to the choir room because he wanted to join choir since the previous year. He really loved to sing, so this wasn't really a new idea for him. He walked into the room and met all the other kids who he had recognized from being in chorus last year, because he would see them arrive to lunch late every day. When you signed up for choir you also volunteered to give up some of your lunch time. The only way they could have choir practice was to have the kids attend chorus twenty minutes a day during their lunch time and then go to eat for the remaining twenty minutes.

The boy loved chorus. He loved to sing and felt he was becoming better and better at it. Through chorus the boy made an exceptional amount of new friends. Friends who actually seemed to like him and not kids who were pretending because he was the sick kid.

At the end of the year, they gave out awards in chorus in random categories. They were little certificates with the person's name on them and the name of the category that the person won. Everyone had voted in chorus a couple weeks prior for the person they believed should win in each category. It turned out that the boy had won the most musical award. The boy was thrilled. This was the award he wanted to win the most. His fellow choristers saw how the boy was always humming or singing some song out loud and how he poured his heart into chorus.

Even though the boy had some good times in chorus he still had to deal with his body being out of whack, especially his metabolism. After the boy had gotten out of the hospital a few months later he gained about fifteen pounds. It might not seem like much to some people, but to a thirteen year old boy who is still developing, it was a big deal. The boy tried to hide his very noticeable weight gain by wearing sweaters all the time. You couldn't catch the boy at anytime in school without a sweater. Even when it was summer and extremely hot outside and inside the school, the boy always had a sweater on.

The boy heard that the school authorities were thinking about making a new school policy where students were not allowed to wear sweaters during the hot summer days to avoid kids overheating or becoming dehydrated. This scared the boy. He didn't want anyone to see how big he actually had become. He was frightened that the school would start introducing this new policy. Fortunately for the boy the school never did enforce such a rule.

During his eighth grade year the boy also wanted to participate in his school's musical. It turned out that the school was doing a show called *Groovy*, which really was about the hippies at Woodstock. The boy was extremely nervous to audition in front of other students and the two instructors. For his audition the boy had chosen to sing "A Whole New World," from *Aladdin*. Some of his fellow choristers and the boy had sung that song in Chorus many times to practice for an ensemble contest between the middle schools. Since the boy had already knew the song he thought that would be easiest for his audition.

The boy sang the song in front of about thirty people in the auditorium. He did alright, not too bad, but not as good as he had wanted to. His nerves had gotten to him. The boy was never ever okay with singing in front of others. It scared him shitless to stand in front of others and sing.

It turned out that the boy won the part of "California

Cowabunga." He was a surfer from California, who was basically doped up with his surfer woman friend and trying to find a place to surf in the middle of an apple field. The boy was shocked at first to find this out. Not that he had gotten a part, but this particular one. He thought his friend Mark should of gotten this part, because he had long, blonde hair and looked more like a surfer than the boy ever could.

The boy even got a second part, a small part at the very beginning of the show and at the end. He had the very first singing lines of the show, which were also the very first lines of the show. This was pretty nerve racking to the boy, but he also felt rather important that he had the very first line of the show and even some of the ending words to the show.

The boy thoroughly loved his time during the musical. There was one embarrassing moment the boy would never forget. During one practice the boy jumped off the front of the stage. Later, they began to rehearse the opening number of the show, where the boy was front and center on stage for the whole song. It was a six or seven minute opening song and scene. It wasn't until after the song that someone stopped and told the boy that there was a giant hole in the back of his pants. The hole was so big that you could see half the boy's leg and underwear. He was so embarrassed and had to continue the rest of the rehearsal wearing his sweater around his waste to cover up the hole. When the boy got home he threw away his pants.

The boy performed in four shows with the cast of *Groovy* and loved every minute of it. The night after his last show, the boy went to go stay with friends of the family for a couple of days, like he often did. He cried and cried because he knew that the show was over and he didn't want it to end. He found a new place where he could be normal and have fun.

It was overall a great year for the boy. Though he had many struggles, the choir, the musical, good grades and new friends made the boy's eighth grade year a good one.

Mental Math

    Entering into his freshmen year the boy wasn't necessarily fat, but a little chubby. Definitely not an obese person, he wanted to lose a few pounds. To address the boy's own personal issues with his weight he took some extreme measures. The boy began keeping a food diary. Each and every day he tracked the calories he'd consumed. The journal he used was an old little notebook given to him by Mrs. Holloway years ago. He never used it before and it pretty much sat around for years. Now he finally had something to use it for. Everyday the boy read every single food label and watched what he ate. Some days the boy would eat five hundred calories or less. At age fifteen and being about five foot ten, the boy should have been consuming about two thousand calories a day. Instead each day the boy was averaging about a thousand calories a day. The boy was indeed starving himself. He would lay around for hours alone in his room, grabbing his stomach that ached with hunger pains and stared at his food diary.

    The boy was clearly beginning to have emerging

symptoms of anorexia. The boy even had a friend at school, Carolyn, who seemed to coin the term "man-orexic" and called the boy that name almost every single day at lunch. The boy almost never ate lunch at school. His friend Carolyn took note everyday that he did not eat lunch and would even make a big deal when he did eat lunch.

Everyday the boy added calories up inside his head. It was a constant fight with the boy and his head. Constantly adding up calories and remembering where he was at in the day. A banana is a 100 calories, plus a slice of pizza which is 350, now he's at 450, then some milk which was about 75 calories now 525. On and on this went every single day. Some days the boy would even be up very late. It was 11:30 and the boy stared at the clock. Since 12:00 am marks a new day, the boy would stare at the clock and wait for the hands to strike 12:00am so he could eat more at the start a new day for his food diary.

He also tried another way of approaching his negative body image. Some days the boy would try to sleep as long as he could to avoid eating. In the boy's head it made total sense to sleep as long as he could so that he could avoid eating throughout the day because he wouldn't wake up until later. The unhealthy eating the boy was indulging in began to take it's toll.

The boy started to have these terrible dizzy spells. He would get up from his bed and go into the hallway and all of a sudden it felt like this force was making his head spin and he became unbalanced. A few times the boy would have fallen over if there wasn't anything to grab on to, luckily, there was always a nearby wall or chair in the boy's house. The boy was unaware of the causes of his dizziness and told his father about them.

After a while, the boy wised up and realized that it was from his lack of eating. Soon after the boy went to the hospital again to see one of his doctors. The boy's dad brought up the issue with the doctor and he refereed him to a new doctor at the same hospital. They ended up seeing the new doctor and all he asked of the boy was to keep a food diary. So for the next week the boy kept a detailed food diary of everything he ate. This was the most unfair week to keep his food diary because it was the boy's grandmother's seventy fifth birthday. Many of his family members were in town. There was plenty of small family parties all week. There was plenty of food for the boy to eat this week and he caved into the temptation of food for the entire week. The boy went back to that new doctor after a week but the boy forgot his food diary. However, the boy's dad assured the doctor that the boy had been eating plenty all week since it was his grandmother's birthday week. After that meeting the boy never saw that doctor again and continued on with his unhealthy eating styles.

    One day, the boy was looking into the mirror with his shirt off and his face expression dropped. The boy had not realized how much weight he had lost till that moment. All of a sudden he was hit with the realization of what happened to him in the last six months. The boy had started at 189 pounds and in six months the boy was 155. The boy could not believe that he was now in the 150's. That always seemed to be unreachable even in any dream he might even try and conjure up.

    One of the nurses at the hospital began to notice the boy's rapid weight loss. The boy's check-ups were about every three to four months at this stage in his life. So, when the nurse took his weight a few months later and the boy was in the 180's and now the nurse weighed him and he was in the 150's. The boy could see her expression changed. Her face flagged this look of worry and concern as if the boy was her son. She began saying things like: "Are you sure you're eating" and "We do have a program here at the hospital, on the same floor as you were on when you were here, for kids who are like this." The boy began to assure her that he was okay and eating just fine. Of course he knew he was lying to her, but it felt as if a part of him even believed in his own lie. There was no way the boy was going to end up on the same fifth floor he was on where he spent so many days during his chemotherapy treatments. No way was he going to be on that same fifth floor that had the most bone-shackling cold atmosphere, with grimace dark hallways at night that gave off that sense of loneliness.

    The boy remembered a day he was there and he met one of the kids on the floor there for nutritional or eating disorder problems. She was a young black girl, with her hair tied back, with glasses and a relatively normal size for a young girl of her age. She wasn't entirely skinny, but she definitely was not fat either. The boy watched her and the nurse from across the hall. There was a table and on it was a plate of food. The young black girl approached the table with the nurse nearby.

    You could tell she had extremely negative feelings toward food and absolutely dreaded the thought of eating. However, the nurse watched as she ate the food, as probably she was supposed to do. You could tell the girl hated it as she sat there drinking juice and taking moderately small bites of food. The boy never wanted to end up like this girl. He would never be confined to that fifth floor again, with nurses watching him from time to time checking on him, making sure he ate. He told himself he'd do whatever convincing that was necessary to persuade the nurse and everyone else around him that he was indeed *fine*. The boy was on this new high sensation of seeing what weight loss was doing for him and was not about to be dragged down from his new self-appointed pedestal.

After a little while the boy did finally stop. He didn't stop because he got help or because anyone came to talk to him about his problem, but merely because he realized what he was doing to himself was harmful. He progressively grew tired of being dizzy all the time, a constant feeling as if his head was racing at a hundred miles and hour and being unbalanced. He also grew tired of doing all the tedious addition in his head., constantly noting and being aware of how many calories were in every little thing he ate.

It also seemed, that after months the boy also grew up. He simply grew up. As he got older and looked through the pages of his food journal, every page he flipped through from start to finish was dated and calorie amounts were recorded. The sight of all these records began to slowly cripple him inside. He didn't want one more single date or calorie to be noted on those pages ever again. After a period of almost seven months the boy stopped his insane eating style. He was amazed at what happened over the last half of the year.

Madame Maxine

His freshmen year also met him with another surgery. See, the gold old bone doctor *fucked* the boy over rather well. See, the doctor put the boy's fake leg in and made it an inch longer than his good leg, the one unaffected by cancer, on purpose. He did this because the boy was only twelve at the time, indeed he was going to still grow. You could also look at the boy's father and see that he was six foot three and the boy at twelve was about five ten.

Not only did the boy's leg eventually grow another inch to be exact with the left leg, but then it proceeded to grow another inch. So now the boy's right leg was longer than his left leg. A much noticeable difference that threw off the boy's body. Now that his legs were uneven again, the boy experienced much pain in his hips and both legs.

To correct this the boy had to go see another doctor at the hospital. The new doctor's name was Dr. Monika Kogan. A woman that looked as if she was in her mid thirties, dark hair and kind of short hair for a woman, She looked white with some kind of random foreign blood that the boy was unable to place. But to the boy, she really looked like Madame Maxine from Harry Potter, which turns out was actually played by a man. Not that she looked like a man, but she looked like a woman character from one of the Harry Potter movies.

    She met with the boy and his father and discussed their options for surgery to correct the boy's problem. The first option was to go into the boy's right leg, purposely break the leg and then they could set the bone any way they way they desired to even out the height. The second option was to go into the right knee and put plates into the boy's leg. These plates would stunt the growth in the boy's right leg so his left leg could catch up and the legs would even out.

    So in November of 2007 the boy had yet another leg surgery. He chose to have the surgery done where the plates were placed into his right knee to stop the growth in his leg. The surgery had left the boy's knee in much pain and it burned like hell. It felt as if someone had lit the boy's leg on fire. Sometimes the boy had to grab his knee and rap his hands around it because it would burn. Many times the boy could not even move or get up because his leg hurt too much.

The boy was now supposed to take a week or two off of school. This was horrible news to the boy. He was now a freshmen in high school. He was not able to afford to miss any school. High school had brought him more homework and school committed time then he had ever had before.

The boy had taken a couple of days off and decided he wanted to go back earlier than initially planned. It was hard for the boy to get around the first couple periods of the day with his crutches. Not because he had crutches, but because his leg was swollen, hurt and burned at many points throughout the day. When the boy got to Spanish class his leg was throbbing in pain. The boy was in real pain and his pain was clearly visible on his face. His teacher easily noticed his pain

His Spanish teacher, Senora Harren, was an older woman,

somewhat zany and a little crazy, but in good ways. She had short, somewhat curled at the ends, brown hair and an appealing smile and personality. She was always a welcoming and enthusiastic person who was a joy to be around. She was an intelligent woman who quickly noted the boy was in distress.

She asked him if he wanted to go to the nurse and go home. But the boy declined and instead agreed to go to the nurse and get some ice for his burning leg and then return to class. The boy went to the nurse's office grabbed some ice and quickly returned to his class. There he sat for a while in class bracing the ice bag against his leg. It now burned less but it still throbbed with pain. After a while the boy sat at the teacher's desk and stretched his leg on a neighboring chair. That way he could extend his leg so it would not be so bent because it always felt better extended than bent.

The boy wrestled to stay at the desk with his leg on another chair, balancing the bag of ice on his leg and trying to take notes. He struggled and struggled with trying to accomplish all of these tasks, but he eventually gave up and told Senora Harren that he would in fact be leaving to go home. He thanked her and said goodbye to a teacher's class he would be missing again.

The boy headed back to the nurses office where he called his father to pick him up. The boy walked outside in his crutches where he waited for his father to arrive. He began to grow tired from standing up on his crutches trying his hardest to balance and not fall over while waiting for his father. When his father finally came, the boy got into the car fast and apologized to his father for having to be picked up. The boy protested that he should of waited a few more days to go back to school. To the boy's surprise the father said very little and actually didn't get mad or yell at the boy, like he was expecting.

The boy and his father drove back home and during the ride home the boy kept thinking about how he should have stayed home and not went to school. He didn't want it to be like the old days where he missed a great deal of his school days, where he totally felt disconnected from school, his friends and from a normal life.

Senior Year

The future moved to the boy's senior year. He turned eighteen and remembered starting the whole hospital experience at the age of twelve. He still couldn't believe it most of the time that his hospital days were over. He is almost done with high school and would start college in the fall. He was amazed at how fast the last four years have flown by. Each and every day he still struggles with the pain in his legs slowing him down and causing him emotional and physical pain and the ugly scars on his legs that show where he's been. His excessive obsession over his weight, his stretch marks, five surgeries and more to come, the disfigured leg, being an inch short on one leg and overall the emotional burden the last six years have been on him. But now he looks up, has a new sense of opportunity and optimism. He's down to one check up a year at the hospital and is finally able to take the burden off of his father.

Easy, Cheap and Close (ECC)

Almost six years later the boy started his first year at college. College was a mind-blowing experience for the boy, as it must be for most people. The boy was in a whole new atmosphere. College was extremely different than high school and much tougher. However, the boy was up for the challenge. The boy decided to stay at home for the first year of college. The boy's local community college, Elgin Community College, was extremely close and cheap. Doing community college for the first year was so much more convenient. The boy already had his job for a year now and could go to school, still work and make money. Elgin Community College was hilariously known as easy, cheap and close: and that it is.

Myths and Realizations

Some say they heard the boys leg crack when he fell six years ago, some say he was pushed and that's why he fell. Jeffrey Kyle Zumbek is the boy's name and he's the only one who knows every single detail of what happened to him over the last six years, and that boy who was once a young twelve year old cancerous kid is me. I am Jeffrey Kyle Zumbek. I struggle each and every day with my past, but I then think to myself *every* day… That sickness made me who I am today, made me appreciate my dad and little things in my life so much more. Things could be worse. I could be in the hospital again but that never ending thought that I can get cancer again doesn't control me, because I now know I can do anything, I have no limits, I have no burdens, I have no fear…. I am finally free.

Epilogue

In June 2011 I went for my annual and final check up. It was the summer of 2011, almost 6 years later after my diagnosis I was pronounced cancer free. My last check up went by extremely fast. At this point I only needed one test and had to quickly see the doctor. My test result turned out normal and my doctor only needed to see if I had any complaints in the last year.

A couple weeks later I received a call to my house. It was the hospital. My grandma picked up the phone. I wasn't home at the moment but later when I got home my grandma told me that I got a phone call from the hospital. She told me it was a lady that called and said that I was completely done with my checkups.

I would no longer have any further checkups. I would no longer have to go back to that hospital ever again in my life. It was such a freeing feeling like a breath of fresh air or the first sip of a fresh cup of coffee.

I now felt even more relieved than I have ever felt before.

I never will fully be ok with my past cancer. It haunts me to this very day, even as I sit here and type this up my scarred legs ache with tremendous pain, my eyes water from the thoughts of my past and all other outcomes and the tragic aftermath.

Even though I know I will never be a hundred percent okay, I know I have never grown so much as a person, never overcome so many obstacles and stared death in the face and conquered one of the most amazing challenges a person can face.

Even though I will never fully be ok, I know that I am ok and am doing so much with my life that would never have been possible if I hadn't not faced the struggles and fought for my life over the past six years.

Letter from the Author

I had many reasons for writing this book, biography, collection of short stories, whatever you want to call it. One of the most important reason was to vent. Over the last few years I have had so many built up emotions ready to burst out of my chest. This was a way for me to deal with some of those feelings and be ok with a dark part of my life. As a result of writing this book, I feel more at ease with myself and comfortable with myself. Next, I hope this would be an outlet for others. Unfortunately, more and more these days you hear of more and more diagnoses of cancer. I hope people diagnosed with cancer can read this book and learn how to cope with the same or similar afflictions. In my life, I have always loved to help people. If this book can help at least one person, my experience was beyond myself.

Have you ever fought for your life? That your life depended on how strong you were and even factors out of your control? It's hard to imagine sometimes that our lives are not always in our control. There were moments when I felt like I was on the edge of death, when I felt completely broken and beaten. Those moments only made me into the person I am today, a strong, caring and beautiful person who finds beauty in every day life.

Dear Savanna,
You are my buttercup!
PANERA!

<3
Jeff B.

Made in the USA
Charleston, SC
21 February 2012